mom *in a* million

MOM IN A MILLION

Compiled by Peggy Jones

An Hachette UK Company
www.hachette.co.uk

Summersdale Publishers
Part of Octopus Publishing Group Limited
Carmelite House
50 Victoria Embankment
LONDON
EC4Y 0DZ
UK

www.summersdale.com

This FSC® label means that materials and other controlled sources used for the product have been responsibly sourced

The authorized representative in the EEA is Hachette Ireland, 8 Castlecourt Centre, Dublin 15, D15 XTP3, Ireland (email: info@hbgi.ie)

Printed and bound in China

ISBN: 978-1-83799-837-1
eISBN: 978-1-83799-818-0

To
From

Thank you for carrying me, birthing me, raising me, supporting me, teaching me and loving me unconditionally!

RIHANNA,
TO HER MOTHER

A MOTHER'S LOVE LIBERATES.

Maya Angelou

THANK YOU
FOR BEING
MY
mom

I've never had more appreciation for anyone in my entire life until I became a mom.

CHRISSY TEIGEN

Being a mother is an attitude, not a biological relation.

Robert A. Heinlein

YOU GAVE ME THE STRENGTH I DIDN'T KNOW I HAD. YOU TAUGHT ME THE TRUE MEANING OF SERENITY AND PEACE.

SERENA WILLIAMS,
TO HER CHILD

HOME IS WHERE MOM IS

MOTHERHOOD
IS A GIFT.

Kim Kardashian

ACCEPTANCE, TOLERANCE, BRAVERY, COMPASSION. THESE ARE THE THINGS MY MOM TAUGHT ME.

LADY GAGA

Mom, everything you do matters

Your laugh, charm, kindness, warmth, love, beauty and sparkle light up every room, everywhere, every time.

FERGIE,
TO HER MOTHER

“

THERE IS NO GREATER LOVE.

Naomi Campbell, on the bond between mother and child

I believe the choice to become a mother is the choice to become one of the greatest spiritual teachers there is.

OPRAH WINFREY

YOU'RE

A

mother

LIKE NO

other!

The greatest love
I've ever known.

Halle Bailey,
on becoming a mother

MOTHERHOOD IS A SOURCE OF JOY EVERY SINGLE DAY, SOMETHING STRONGER THAN EVERYTHING ELSE.

CHARLIZE THERON

Your love surrounds ME

THE MOST BEAUTIFUL WORD ON THE LIPS OF MANKIND IS THE WORD "MOTHER".

Kahlil Gibran

WHEN YOU LOOK INTO YOUR MOTHER'S EYES, YOU KNOW THAT IS THE PUREST LOVE YOU CAN FIND ON THIS EARTH.

MITCH ALBOM

Art is the child of nature; yes, her darling child, in whom we trace, the features of the mother's face.

HENRY WADSWORTH LONGFELLOW

ALL THAT I AM I OWE TO *you*

I KISS THE GROUND SHE WALKS ON!

Emma Roberts, on her mother

My son entered this world and my heart grew twice the size.

JESSIE J

YOUR WORDS COMFORT ME, YOUR HUGS HEAL ME AND YOUR LOVE GUIDES ME

My angel babies have shown me a love that I never even knew could run so deep.

Paris Hilton

THERE REALLY ARE PLACES IN THE HEART YOU DON'T EVEN KNOW EXIST UNTIL YOU LOVE A CHILD.

ANNE LAMOTT

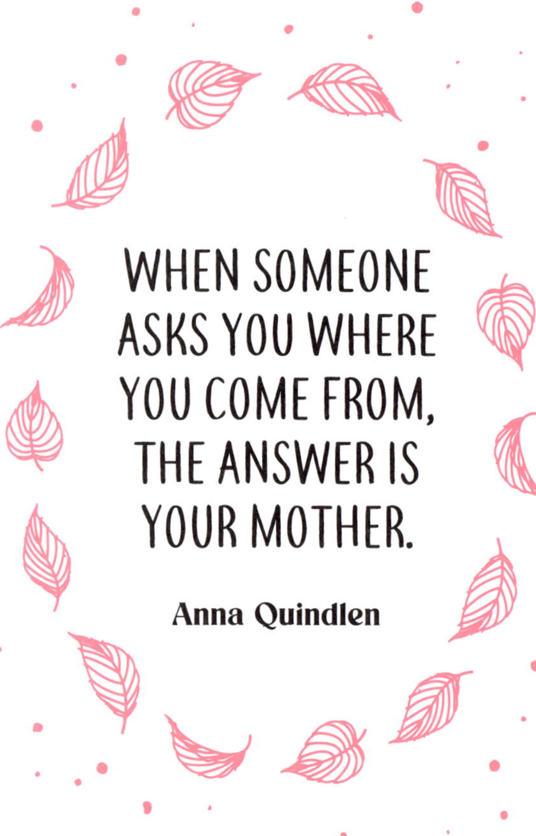

WHEN SOMEONE ASKS YOU WHERE YOU COME FROM, THE ANSWER IS YOUR MOTHER.

Anna Quindlen

My life is wonderful with you in it!

MOTHERHOOD IS THE GREATEST THING AND THE HARDEST THING.

RICKI LAKE

My mother was my role model before I even knew what the word was.

LISA LESLIE

YOUR

love

WAS THERE FROM THE BEGINNING, AND IT HAS NO

“

I AM BECAUSE OF YOU.

Viola Davis, to her mother

”

I wouldn't trade this for anything in the world.

SALMA HAYEK,
ON MOTHERHOOD

The morning after I gave birth, I felt like my whole life had started over.

Jennifer Lawrence

You're never too old to need your MOM

MY MOTHER!
SHE IS BEAUTIFUL,
SOFTENED AT
THE EDGES AND
TEMPERED WITH
A SPINE OF
STEEL. I WANT TO
GROW OLD AND
BE LIKE HER.

JODI PICOULT

THE LOVE FROM YOUR CHILDREN IS CONSTANT AND UNCONDITIONAL.

Katy Perry

YOU'RE
DOING AN
AMAZING
job!

THE ART OF MOTHERING IS TO TEACH THE ART OF LIVING TO CHILDREN.

ELAINE HEFFNER

A mother always has to think twice, once for herself and once for her child.

SOPHIA LOREN

THANK YOU FOR INSPIRING ME ENDLESSLY.

Ariana Grande, to her mother

I FEEL BLESSED TO HAVE YOU AS MY MOM

The natural state of motherhood is unselfishness.

JESSICA LANGE

Once you're a mom, you're always a mom. It's like riding a bike, you never forget.

Taraji P. Henson

Thank you
for all that
you are
and all that
you do

YOU ARE THE EPITOME OF STRENGTH AND GRACE.

KERRY WASHINGTON,
TO HER MOTHER

MOTHER'S LOVE
IS BLISS, IS PEACE,
IT NEED NOT BE
ACQUIRED, IT NEED
NOT BE DESERVED.
Erich Fromm

**MY TEACHER,
MY BESTIE,
MY PARTNER,
MY INSPIRATION.**

ALICIA KEYS,
TO HER MOTHER

YOU INSPIRE
ME TO BE THE
best
VERSION OF
myself

It doesn't matter how old you are or what you do in your life; you never stop needing your mom.

KATE WINSLET

“

SHE PUSHED ME TO FOLLOW MY DREAM.

Gregory Porter, on his mother

Your love makes anything
POSSIBLE

My mom is a strong woman and I love her for it.

TOM HIDDLESTON

The memory of my mother will always be a blessing to me.

Thomas A. Edison

I COULDN'T BE MORE GRATEFUL TO BE A MOM. IT'S BEEN THE BIGGEST BLESSING LIFE HAS OFFERED ME.

LINDSAY LOHAN

I'M THANKFUL TO YOU FOR GIVING ME LIFE, LOVE AND

laughter

YOU KNOW INNATELY WHAT YOUR CHILD NEEDS. YOU SHOULD TRUST THAT.

Lucy Liu, to mothers

A MOTHER IS A
MOTHER STILL,
THE HOLIEST
THING ALIVE.

SAMUEL TAYLOR COLERIDGE

THANK YOU FOR SHOWING ME THE WAY

She is my rock and has been there in the brightest and darkest of times. Her love steadfast and support unwavering.

LUPITA NYONG'O,
ON HER MOTHER

“

WE’RE ALL EVOLVING. I ALWAYS SEE THAT WITH MY KIDS.

Laura Prepon

She is a matriarch, she loves and is loved. She is in charge.

KEIRA KNIGHTLEY,
ON HER MOTHER

Thank you
for always
believing
in me

Life began with waking up and loving my mother's face.

George Eliot

MOM – LOVE IS A FACT LIKE THAT – IT JUST HAPPENS, WHATEVER YOU DO, YOU CAN'T DO ANYTHING ABOUT IT, LIKE RAIN.

KATY REGAN

YOU ARE A
CONSTANT SOURCE OF
strength
AND SUPPORT IN MY
life

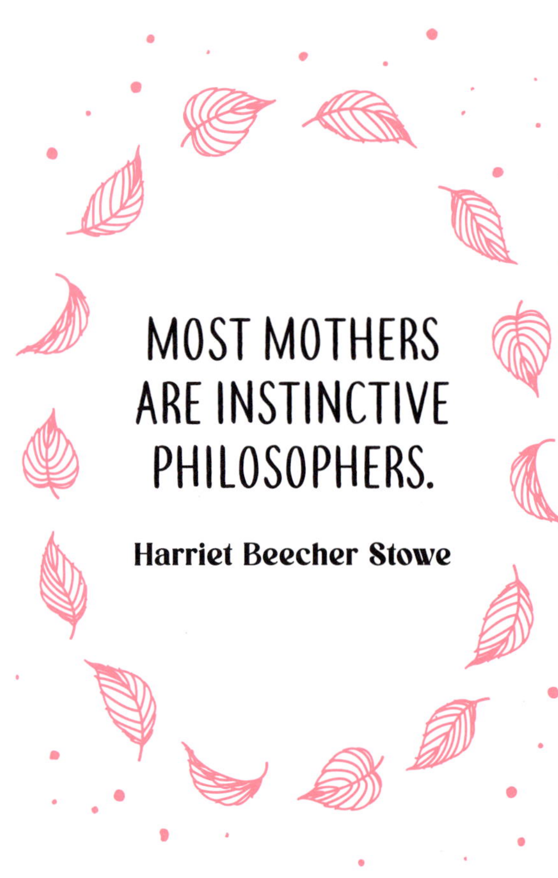

MOST MOTHERS ARE INSTINCTIVE PHILOSOPHERS.

Harriet Beecher Stowe

A MOTHER KNOWS WHAT HER CHILD'S GONE THROUGH, EVEN IF SHE DIDN'T SEE IT HERSELF.

PRAMOEDYA ANANTA TOER

It's just the best thing in the world, being a mom.

MIRANDA KERR

You have a beautiful SOUL

“BEING A MAMA IS A JOB LIKE NO OTHER.

Gigi Hadid

It's the greatest thing I've ever done.

PRIYANKA CHOPRA, ON BECOMING A MOTHER

YOU MAKE THE HARDEST JOB IN THE WORLD

easy

A mother's arms are more comforting than anyone else's.

Diana, Princess of Wales

YOU ARE
THE HEART OF
YOUR FAMILIES,
THE ONES
WHO NURTURE,
GUIDE AND LOVE
UNCONDITIONALLY.

KRIS JENNER,
ON MOTHERS

IT'S AN ACT OF INFINITE OPTIMISM.

Gilda Radner, on motherhood

YOU
LIFT ME
UP AND
LET ME
KNOW
I'M
LOVED

BECOMING A MOTHER CHANGES EVERYTHING.

ADRIANA LIMA

Hugs are very important. I keep saying that to my children.

CATHERINE,
PRINCESS OF WALES

You accept me for who I am

KIDS TEACH YOU TO BE A BETTER HUMAN.

Kelly Clarkson

A mother's arms are made of tenderness and children sleep soundly in them.

VICTOR HUGO

It has shifted everything about me. It has only enriched me.

Jodie Turner-Smith, on motherhood

I'M SO LUCKY
TO HAVE
you
IN MY
life

IF LOVE IS
SWEET AS A
FLOWER, THEN
MY MOTHER IS
THAT SWEET
FLOWER
OF LOVE.

STEVIE WONDER

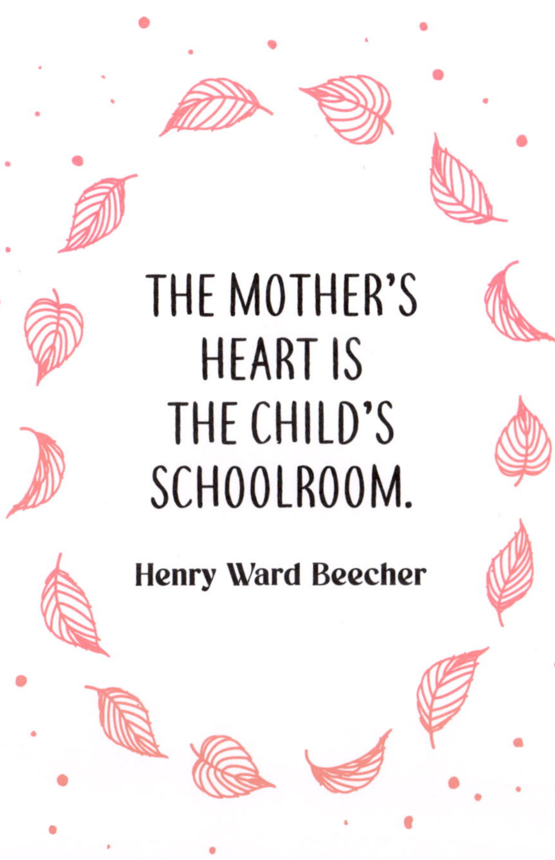
THE MOTHER'S
HEART IS
THE CHILD'S
SCHOOLROOM.
Henry Ward Beecher

Thank you for everything you've done for me and everything YOU STILL DO

WHEN I CLOSE MY EYES AND VISUALIZE MY MOTHER, I SEE PURE BEAUTY.

KATE HUDSON

**Being a mom
is the most
incredible thing
I've ever done.**

PINK

“

HE MAKES ME SO
PROUD OF MYSELF.

Adele, on her son

YOU WORK

miracles

For me, motherhood is learning about the strengths I didn't know I had.

HALLE BERRY

I owe her everything.

Denzel Washington, on his mother

NOBODY'S
GOT A
MOM
QUITE
LIKE
MINE!

WHO RAN TO HELP ME WHEN I FELL, AND WOULD SOME PRETTY STORY TELL, OR KISS THE PLACE TO MAKE IT WELL? MY MOTHER.

ANN TAYLOR

EVERYTHING IS NEW AGAIN.

Hilary Swank, on having children

THE HEART OF A MOTHER IS A DEEP ABYSS AT THE BOTTOM OF WHICH YOU WILL ALWAYS FIND FORGIVENESS.

HONORÉ DE BALZAC

You show me the path and help me on my way

Thank you for being you and all that you are. A guiding light. A loving heart and a generous soul.

BELLA HADID,
TO HER MOTHER

“

MY MOTHER HAS ALWAYS BEEN MY EMOTIONAL BAROMETER AND MY GUIDANCE.

Emma Stone

THANK YOU

FOR

always

BEING

OPEN-MINDED

Being a parent has made me more open, more connected to myself, more happy and more creative.

ALICIA KEYS

Grown don't mean nothing to a mother. A child is a child.

Toni Morrison

THE BEST JOB THAT I'VE EVER HAD IS BEING A MOTHER.

TINA KNOWLES

YOU MEAN
SO MUCH TO
me

I DIDN'T KNOW HOW MUCH LOVE I HAD IN ME.

Katie Holmes, on becoming a mother

MOTHERS ARE THE VITAL WARMTH OF SUN – AND THEY ARE THE COMFORTING COOLNESS OF SHADE.

TERRI GUILLEMETS

Your love is

POWERFUL

A mother is one to whom you hurry when you are troubled.

EMILY DICKINSON

MOTHERHOOD: ALL LOVE BEGINS AND ENDS THERE.

Robert Browning

I love my kids more than anything. I cannot imagine not being a parent.

HILARY DUFF

I KNOW HOW TO LOVE BECAUSE OF YOU

Sometimes the strength of motherhood is greater than natural laws.

Barbara Kingsolver

A MOTHER'S LOVE FOR HER CHILD IS LIKE NOTHING ELSE IN THE WORLD.

AGATHA CHRISTIE

You're everything I could ever ask for in a mom

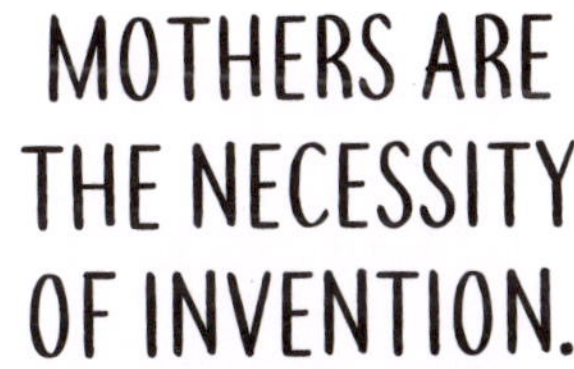

MOTHERS ARE
THE NECESSITY
OF INVENTION.

Bill Watterson

ALL THOSE CLICHÉS, THOSE THINGS YOU HEAR ABOUT HAVING A BABY AND MOTHERHOOD – ALL OF THEM ARE TRUE.

PENÉLOPE CRUZ

At the end of the day, my most important job is still mom-in-chief.

MICHELLE OBAMA

SAFETY IS IN YOUR ARMS, STRENGTH IS IN YOUR *hands*

AND WISDOM IS IN YOUR *footsteps*

"A MOTHER IS THE TRUEST FRIEND WE HAVE."

Washington Irving

Motherhood has a very humanizing effect. Everything gets reduced to essentials.

MERYL STREEP

You are always there for

ME

We all have our own ways of how we mother our kids, and that's what makes us all uniquely us.

Ciara

I WILL ACCEPT LOTS OF THINGS, BUT NOT WHEN SOMEONE INSULTS MY MOM, THE NICEST PERSON IN THE WORLD.

ANDY MURRAY

YOU DON'T HAVE TO BE A SPECIFIC TYPE OF MOM TO BE A GREAT MOM.

Jennifer Lopez

YOU ARE THE STRONGEST PERSON I *know*

MY DAUGHTER INTRODUCED ME TO MYSELF.

BEYONCÉ

Only mothers can think of the future – because they give birth to it in their children.

MAXIM GORKY

YOU
WERE
ALWAYS
DESTINED
TO BE
MY MOM

I HAVE SO MUCH COMPASSION – AND LOVE AND APPRECIATION – FOR ALL MOTHERS IN THE WORLD.

Cardi B

This is the most fulfilling thing that I've ever done in my life.

CAMERON DIAZ,
ON BECOMING A MOTHER

My mother
is my root,
my foundation.
She planted the
seed that I base
my life on.

Michael Jordan

The love
you show me
I deserve is
deep, powerful
and true

THE MOST IMPORTANT TITLE I WILL EVER HAVE IS “MOM”.

MEGHAN MARKLE

MY SOUL IS COMPLETE BECAUSE OF YOU.
Khloé Kardashian, to her children

THANK YOU FOR
ALWAYS FINDING TIME,
energy
AND LOVE FOR
me

SHE LOVED ME SO UNCONDITIONALLY, IN A WAY NO ONE ELSE EVER WILL AND THAT IS FOREVER.

RASHIDA JONES,
ON HER MOTHER

Mother is the name for God in the lips and hearts of little children.

WILLIAM MAKEPEACE THACKARAY

"THE KIND OF POWER MOTHERS HAVE IS ENORMOUS.

Angela Carter

Mom,
you're my
SOULMATE

The greatest pain I've ever known and the greatest accomplishment that I've ever achieved.

ASHLEY GRAHAM,
ON GIVING BIRTH

Motherhood has taught me patience and the power of unconditional love.

Karlie Kloss

YOUR LOVE IS MY LOVE, THAT'S HOW I KNOW IT'LL NEVER

end

THE MOST IMPORTANT THING I'VE DONE, THE BIGGEST THING I'VE DONE, IS BECOME A MOTHER.

JANET JACKSON

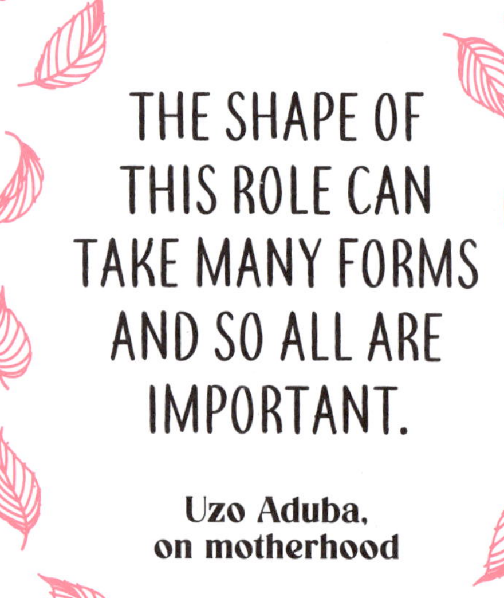

THE SHAPE OF THIS ROLE CAN TAKE MANY FORMS AND SO ALL ARE IMPORTANT.

Uzo Aduba,
on motherhood

A MOTHER IS NOT A PERSON TO LEAN ON, BUT A PERSON TO MAKE LEANING UNNECESSARY.

DOROTHY CANFIELD FISHER

MOM, YOU'RE MAGICAL TO ME

Yes, Mother. I can see you are flawed. You have not hidden it. That is your greatest gift to me.

ALICE WALKER

“YOU GROW TOGETHER.

Angelina Jolie, on raising children

You always go above and beyond for me, and for that I'm eternally grateful

Pride is one of the seven deadly sins; but it cannot be the pride of a mother in her children.

CHARLES DICKENS

My mom was always my friend. Always.

Taylor Swift

MOTHER IS
A VERB, NOT
A NOUN.

SHONDA RHIMES

THERE'S NO WAY TO BE A PERFECT MOTHER AND A MILLION WAYS TO BE A GOOD ONE.

Jill Churchill

BIRTH IS THE EPICENTER OF WOMEN'S POWER.

ANI DiFRANCO

I'LL
ALWAYS
BE IN AWE
OF YOU

Have you enjoyed this book?

If so, find us on Facebook at **Summersdale Publishers**, on Twitter/X at **@Summersdale** and on Instagram, TikTok and Bluesky at **@summersdalebooks** and get in touch.

We'd love to hear from you!

www.summersdale.com

IMAGE CREDITS

Leaves throughout © NIKHOMKEDBAN/Shutterstock.com; continuous line-drawing heart © Maria_Galybina/Shutterstock.com